...d on or before

KT-442-960

An Ear to the Ground

STEWART CONN

An Ear to the Ground

HUTCHINSON OF LONDON

00439 9163

HUTCHINSON & CO (*Publishers*) LTD
3 Fitzroy Square, London W1

London Melbourne Sydney Auckland
Wellington Johannesburg Cape Town
and agencies throughout the world

First published 1972

821
CON

*This book has been set in Bembo type, printed in Great Britain
on cartridge paper by Anchor Press, and
bound by Wm. Brendon, both of Tiptree, Essex*

ISBN 0 09 11080 7

'Marriage a Mountain Ridge' first appeared in *Poetry* (Chicago). Other poems have appeared or are due to appear in *Ariel*, *The Critical Quarterly*, *International Review*, *Lines Review*, *The Listener*, *New Statesman*, *Poetry Review*, *The Scotsman*, *Scottish International*, *Transatlantic Review*, *Wave* and on BBC Radio 3.

Acknowledgment is also made to the editors of *Contemporary Scottish Verse* (Calder and Boyars), *Scottish Poetry* (Edinburgh University Press), *The Young British Poets* (Chatto and Windus) and *Modern Poets in Focus* (Corgi).

'Message from an Island' was commissioned by the National Book League.

Contents

One

Kilchrenan

Looking out on Cruachan, the church is whitewashed:
Monuments to McIntyre and McCorquedale

Kept simple, Cailean Mor's sword set in stone.
The old days would see some cold funerals.

As always, the gentry dominate. Two lofts
Used to face each other, where the lairds

Sat crossing glances, smouldering slowly
Under their ordered curls . . . the sermon droning.

See them descend, their ladies in lace,
Then jog arrogantly off, leaving behind

An odour of musk and Madeira, where now sheep
Go blindly nudging clumps of daffodils.

Crippled Aunt

As the sermon draws to a close, I glance
　　Across at you through dusty chutes of light.
　　　　The pews are golden. You sit
Padded with cushions, as in a trance:
Safe from the Devil and his vigorous dance.

Outside the bright world hums—no hive
　　Brimming with honey, but traffic
　　　　Bound for the coast. A truck
(Like the one that struck you?) drives
Past, stressing the miracle of your being alive.

You used to worship, on unbroken knees,
　　In a village chapel with honeysuckle
　　　　Ladling the air. I still
Have snapshots of you, among the roses.
God's will has strange ironies.

Such energy and gracefulness were yours
　　It is baffling to see you sit
　　　　Paralysed to the waist yet
Worshipping God who took your gay colours,
With a faith so elemental, fierce.

Watching them wheel you down the aisle, I am humble.
　　I, who would curse the fate
　　　　That has twisted you into what
You are, shudder to hear you say life's ample
For your needs, Christian by such example.

On Craigie Hill

The farmhouse seems centuries ago,
The steadings slouched under a sifting of snow
For weeks on end, lamps hissing, logs stacked
Like drums in the shed, the ice having to be cracked
To let the shaggy cats drink. Or
Back from the mart through steaming pastures
Men would come riding—their best
Boots gleaming, rough tweeds pressed
To a knife-edge, pockets stuffed with notes.

Before that even, I could visualise (from coloured
Prints) traps rattling, wheels spinning; furred
Figures posing like sepia dolls
In a waxen world of weddings and funerals.
When Todd died, last of the old-stagers,
Friends of seventy years followed the hearse.
Soon the farm went out of the family: the Cochranes
Going to earth or, like their cousins,
Deciding it was time to hit town.

The last link broken, the farm-buildings stand
In a clutter below the quarry. The land
Retains its richness—but in other hands.
Kilmarnock has encroached. It is hard to look
Back with any sense of belonging.
Too much has changed, is still changing.
This blustery afternoon on Craigie Hill
I regard remotely the muddy track
My father used to trudge along, to school.

The Lilypond

I stand at the edge of the lilypond
With its swart fronds
And submerged stems. Scarcely defined
Forms nudge the surface and dip back down.

Years ago, I seem to remember, the water
Was clear; the leaves green saucers
You wanted to walk on. Beyond,
The hot-house. Now its spars

Are smashed, the iron flamingoes
Gone. One day soon, the pond
Is to be drained. I shall not be here.
Better simply arrive and find

The area filled in, than see
The process as I imagine it:
Orange shapes with white
Growths being scooped out

By men in rubber gloves;
Then speedily disposed of.
I'd be free to surmise
The stench, the bunches of flies.

In so many ways, we avoid
Being in at the death;
Preferring to let nature take its course,
And putting in an appearance

When we know all is safe.
Again and again I am drawn
Here, to the lilypond.
Elsewhere, there is hurt enough.

Sisters

Brought up in Barnton, they shared
A sheltered girlhood, with moments
To look back on: a trip to Paris
With the doctor's family down the road,
The odd dance, hiking holidays
In Mull. As they matured, one leaned
Towards bookishness, ending up
Married to someone intellectually
Her superior but who recognised
Purer qualities when they came his way.
The other, by contrast, met
A handsome devil who fell
For the flappers—so that all
She could do was put the pieces
Together and take up a career.
Now, forty years later,
They are back in Edinburgh
A stone's throw from each other.
The younger casts an envious eye
On her sister—with a man
About the house, family to visit,
Security and fulfilment around her:
While she in return has a diary
With more than she can cope with;
Freedom, friends, fancy furniture.
Each thinks she prefers her sister's lot,
And makes no bones about it. Yet neither,
For all she wants, would give up what she's got.

Old Actor

Not the same nowadays. They don't play
Shakespeare properly—not the way
We used to. Too superior
For a frontcloth, that's their

Trouble. Opera use it, why not Theatre?
I mean, take the first scene from 'Caesar'—
That ought to be done out front, the main
Area set for the procession.

As for 'Hamlet', a gravedigger here
Or there hardly matters any more.
(I saw Benson, as the Prince,
Carried off after 'The rest is silence'—

But that *improved* the text.) Donat,
Martin-Harvey . . . what *style*. Another thing,
We'd always an orchestra in the pit
For the Bard—not a gramophone in the wings.

Stage effects too: real waterfalls,
You name it—even Skegness,
Still the gas-floats. All they want these
Days in a lad is, well you know . . . *balls*.

Not that I'm against manliness,
Anything of the sort. Bawdry, for that matter.
I just think there are other
Things that count, besides filling a codpiece.

Journeying North

Leaving Carlisle, the diesel pulls
Uphill, till a signal falls
And we put on speed.
                That morning
I'd seen the Magritte exhibition
At the Tate. One portrait,
Of a couple kissing through sacking,
Put me in mind of Darnley
In his taffeta mask, then of our
Fumbling devotion.
                Out there,
The slack reaches of Solway.

Another, more sinister,
Had two Edwardian figures
With a club and a net;
A nude on a bed,
Her mouth pouring blood.

Hurtling north, my fears
Are of a different order:
Imagining you laying my meal
On a frail cloth that might
Have been a bridal veil,
I consider the split cell,
The unruly corpuscle
In the gallery of the skull . . .

The air thick with tobacco-smoke
We near Gretna. Heavy anvils strike.

Émigrée

A young girl in a faded photograph,
You sit delicately holding a fur muff:
Wistful yet wary, as though you already know
What winters await you, what habitual snow;
What unheated rooms and visits to the dacha
(Funeral bells tolling), what journeys on the Volga
In late spring, the pack-ice melting . . .

I imagine you trying out your halting
English on the servants; starting at a frown
On a familiar face, an icon staring down.
You are to escape all this, leaving behind
The women in black, the massive chambers
With their velvet curtains, the great chandeliers—
And outside, cannon firing along the frontiers
Of Europe. How you have changed over the years . . .

But I realise that what you have retained
Is a stunning sharpness of eye and mind.
Seeing through our masculine conjuring-tricks
A lesser concern, your ear is attuned
To the distant whistling of a more brutal axe.

Summer Afternoon

She spends the afternoon in a deckchair,
Not moving, a handkerchief over
Her head. From the end of the garden
Her eyes look gouged. The children stare,
Then return to their game. She used to take
Them on country walks, or swimming in the lake.
These days are gone, and will not come again.

Dazzling slats of sunlight on the lawn
Make her seem so vulnerable; her bombazine
Costume fading with each drifting beam.
As the children squall, she imagines
Other generations: Is that you, Tom,
Or Ian, is it?—forgetting one was blown
To bits at Ypres, the other on the Somme.

Momentarily in pain, she tightens
Her lips into something like a grin.
There comes the first rustle of rain.
Carrying her in, you avoid my eye
For fear of interception, as who should say
Shall we, nearing extremity,
Be equal objects of distaste and pity?

Yet desperate in the meantime to forbear
For the sake of the love this poor
Creature bore us, who was once so dear.

Tutorial

'Leaving aside Fielding's peculiarly national
Style, let us trace the novel

Through Miss Austen: observation
Allied to wit, a feminine intuition . . .'

With pleasing prejudice and pride
We take a cabriolet-ride

Down sunny lanes (bypassing Thackeray,
And Scott's drayhorse, on the way).

Tempting though it is to drink in
The country setting, the formal scenes,

I keep seeing those metal wheels spin—
And a young girl, composed, holding the reins.

The King

They scoured me and laid me
On two boards, supported by trestles.
Head facing east, arms crossed.

Then lowered me
Into place, lighting candles
Before sealing the mouth of the cave.

My hair tied to an oak beam;
The rest of my body
Enveloped in hazel leaves.

On the walls, like tapestries,
The pelts of hounds, heads
Hinged, jaws grinning.

And alongside, the two youngest
Of my wives, breasts bared,
Gashes in their throats:

Already the air filches
Them, wrist and ankle
Contained by a green flame.

At my side, pitchers of wine
And water, trays of sweetmeats,
Barrels of honey and lard.

And my broadsword polished
So that it dazzles, the haft
Within easy reach of my fist.

These apart I have cushions
For comfort, silver coins,
Scrolls for a long hour, a horn

To waken the dead. But
I lie here, my skull still split.
So far, nothing has happened.

Forbears

My father's uncle was the fastest
Thing on two wheels, sitting in a gig,
The reins tight, his back at an angle
Of thirty degrees, puffing up dust-clouds
As he careered down Craigie Hill.

His father before him, the strongest man
In Ayrshire, took a pair of cartwheels
By the axle and walked off with them. I have
Visions of him in the meadow, holding
Two ropes, a stallion straining on each.

Before that, no doubt, we boasted
The straightest furrow, the richest yield.
No measurement needed: each farm
Bore its best, as each tree its fruit.
We even had a crazy creature in crinolines

Who locked her letters in a brass box.
Others too . . . But what do such truths
 Add up to—when the nearest
(And furthest) I get is visiting
Their elaborate, uncared-for graves?

On an adjoining stone are a skull
And hourglass, from Covenanter
Days. Their lives were a duller
Sacrifice. John on his moral staff,
The great-aunts with their rigid ways,

Smacking of goodness in the strictest
Sense, members of a sect, Elect almost,
Shared surely something of flint
In the brain. Sad, that their mortal goal
Was salvation, not purification of the soul.

Farm Funeral

His hearse should have been drawn by horses.
That's what he envisaged: the strain
And clop of crupper and chain, flashing
Brass, fetlocks forcing high. With below
Him, the frayed sheets turning slowly yellow.

On the sideboard a silver cup he had won,
Inscribed 'to Todd Cochrane', now a lamp;
And tinted prints of his trotting days,
Switch in hand, jockey-capped, the gig silky
With light, wheels exquisitely spinning.

For fifty years he was a breeder of horses;
Nursing them nightly, mulling soft praise
Long after the vet would have driven his plunger in.
Yet through them was his hip split. Twice
He was crushed by a stallion rearing.

Himself to the end unbroken. God's tool, yes,
That to earth will return. But not before time.
He ought to have been conveyed to the grave
By clattering Clydesdales, not cut off
From lark and sorrel by unseemly glass.

The shire is sprinkled with his ashes.
The fields are green through his kind. Their clay,
His marrow. As much as the roisterer, he: even
That last ride to Craigie, boots tightly laced,
His tie held in place by a diamond pin.

The Predators

—a sequence

1

From Aquitaine, its turrets and towers
Yellow with age, limestone lashed
By the sun, its baked pantiles

And fig-groves, Isaiah's robe flowing
Like flame; in the path
Of de Montfort's sordid plunder

We rise through layer upon layer
Of spiders-webs white in the mist;
By train, follow the gorge

(Lines forged in red rock),
Then by bus track the causse
Toward Conques. The last miles on foot.

2

As, parched and footsore, pilgrims
For Compostella climbed to the spring,
Fed and huddled in the clerestory for warmth:

Who in times past had left no alms—
Till a brother purloined from a nearby
Abbey the relics of Ste Foy.

Thereafter, the church built. Cool
Cloisters, the fountains stuffed with pike,
A vault in due course added

To the tympanum with its carved
Angels and Devils, eyes
Pierced, a Last Judgment in stone.

3
During the Revolution the church treasure
Divided for safe keeping, among
The peasants; later gathered in, no item

Missing.
            Including the great cross,
Tapestries depicting the Saint's
Decapitation at the hands

Of the Romans.
            Also her likeness
In beaten gold, enthroned and bedizened
With intaglios from the faithful (penitents

And others)—Marcus Aurelius
In agate; Aeneas, the deepest
Jade; Caligula all jowls and curls.

4
Yet the treasure unseemly,
Under its glass case. Nothing prim
In the mouth (as most Saints)

But a hard line. The blue eyes, enamel.
Barbaric, that the relics of a child
Should have lain within this cocoon.

In the church, dust drips.
The choir-rails are spiked.
Here too the spiders are at work.

The pulpit is meshed in web. High
Overhead a bird that has flown in
Beats silently from beam to beam.

5
Outside, on a hill track,
I reach a mica-ridge: coil
Of flesh to tilt of bone.

Three huntsmen pass a station
Of the cross. Their barrels
Flash; the rabbits' heads

Swell. Here 'were rounded up
And set before a firing-squad
In the public square (by way

Of reprisal) all members
Of the local Resistance, June '44'—
Having been first betrayed.

6
Much earlier, the impact of Rome:
Caesar persuading the Gauls
Their gods had abandoned them

And, for delaying his conquest,
Having the right hand of each male
Struck off.
            Under Dacian

The martyrdom for her faith
Of Ste Foy.
            Since when the wheel
Has turned: the slit corpses

Of Protestants choking the well
At Penne; Coligny himself
Exacting the most atrocious revenge.

7
Notwithstanding, the church
Faces the chestnut slopes,
The vineyards beyond. Human vice depicted

In sculpted stone. At the centre,
That idol in gold. A lay-brother
Leads crowds of tourists

From the garth. In the nave
All is silent. My eyes
Are drawn up and up. Layers

Of light stream through the vault.
The bird beats itself senseless
Against the stone. Below, the webs wait.

Three

Escapologist

He operates not so much by muscular
Strength (though that counts) as sheer

Intensity of will. For a long time he strains
Against the grid of padlocks and chains,

Chest rising as he prises each loop
Open, finally giving cold steel the slip

As a salmon might a net. Despite
This, we suspect he is a cheat;

The whole act a put-up job. What we really
Resent is the visionary gleam in his eye

As he steps clear of the last link: our applause
Is grudging, because natural laws

Are being broken. Yet I know a man
Who lives on an island, in one room—

And whose poetry bends bars of iron.

A Sense of Order

Sunday Walk
I stop at the foot of Garioch Drive
Where my aunt used to live
Three floors up.
                    I remember the smell
Of camomile that hit you in the hall,
The embroidered sampler, the jars
Of wax chrysanths, the budgerigars
In their lacquered cage; the ladies who came
To read the Bible in the front room—
Surrounded by marzipan, and dragons
On silky screens.
                    A rag-and-bone man,
His pony ready for the knacker's yard,
Rounds a corner (short of a tail-light)
And disappears up Clouston Street.

Below, the Kelvin runs like stinking lard.

Period Piece
Hand in hand, the girls glide
Along Great Western Road.
                              Outside
The Silver Slipper the boys wait,
Trousers flared, jacket-pockets
Bulging with carry-outs.

The girls approach. A redhead pouts,
Sticks her tongue out,
Then passes under the strung lights
To the dance-floor. 'I'll have it
Off with that one.' 'Want to bet?'
'I'd rather lumber her mate . . .'

They nick their cigarettes.
                                    Inside,
The miniskirts are on parade,
Listening to The Marmalade.

Cranworth Street
I climb the tenement stair
With its scoured tiles, its odour
Of cat.
          We lived here, before
My father moved to Ayrshire.
I have not been back, for years.

The brass nameplate, the square
Bellpull, mean nothing any more.
What is there to recapture,
To rediscover? It is too late
In the season, for that.

I cling to the wooden
Rail and, for no reason,
Break out in a sweat
As I reach the street.

Street Scene
The faces outside the Curlers
Explode like fat cigars
In the frosty air.

Even the newspaper-seller
Rocks on his heels, half-seas over.
And I don't blame him.

As the pictures
Come out, scores of lovers
Head for their parked cars.

Two ladies whisper
Goodnight to each other.
Neither feels secure
Till on her own stair
She snibs the basement door
And breathes freely, behind iron bars.

Tremors

We took turns at laying
An ear on the rail—
So that we could tell
By the vibrations

When a train was coming.
Then we'd flatten ourselves
To the banks, scorched
Vetch and hedge-parsley,

While the iron flanks
Rushed past, sending sparks
Flying. It is more and more
A question of living

With an ear to the ground:
The tremors, when they come,
Are that much greater—
For ourselves, and others.

Nor is it any longer
A game, but a matter
Of survival: each explosion
Part of a procession

There can be no stopping.
Though the end is known,
There is nothing for it
But to keep listening . . .

Suicide

She could have thrown
Herself in front of a train
In her local station, and been prised off the line
By 'a little man with a bar of iron'.

Alternatives were the gas oven,
An overdose, a knife in the vein
Done in the heat of passion.
Instead she arrived alone

By plane, paid her fare
To the island and began
Walking across the stunted heather
Towards Rackwick. Where the bare

Cliffs were steepest, she stepped over.
They found her, every bone
Broken, the pelvis driven to the shoulder.
Why go to such bother

When other ways seem simpler?
How such inhuman composure?
Was she irresistibly drawn
Here or was it, like Karenin, a question

Of heaping error on error
To put an end to torture—
Begging, as she went down,
That she might be forgiven?

Portents

Southpark
The area palls, and its mildewed parades.
  Victorian terraces,
 Taken over for the University, lose
Their ironwork, their fluted balustrades.

Among the charred bedsteads, the crazy mirrors,
  I keep thinking of those men in dungarees
 Putting an axe through Mackintosh's
Front door . . . Glasgow is in arrears.

The Salon
The supporting programme always began
At 5.30. But they didn't open
  Till 5.28. So that
 By the time you'd got your ticket
  And found your seat
You'd missed the first four minutes.

Once when we could scarcely see the screen
  For fog, we didn't complain—
 But sat through the entire programme again:
  Phantom cops, after a phantom Keaton.

 In December, the gate
 Was locked. The white
Frontage peels. The posters are gone
But for a clutch of curls, a crimped grin.

Costume Piece
Every morning, two women in Edwardian costume
Stood for hours opposite the men's Union.

It seemed one or other had been let down
By a medical student: clear water over sharp stones.

When they disappeared, I hoped for a happy
Conclusion—only to hear both had been put away.

Botanics
Somewhere, a clock strikes. Schoolboys
    In cherry caps and corduroys
Face the deathtrap of Great Western Road
    Watched by a lollipop-man; then head

For the ice-cream parlour
    And the Gardens—where the keeper,
Not wanting trouble, goes inside
    To his prize orchids, his marble nudes.

Behind the hothouse the boys shout
    At an artist in sombrero and tights
Too dour even to look up. By the gate
    The winnowing fantails preen and pirouette.

Family Visit

Laying linoleum, my father spends hours
With his tape measure,
Littering the floor
As he checks his figures, gets
The angle right; then cuts
Carefully, to the music
Of a slow logic. In despair
I conjure up a room where
A boy sits and plays with coloured bricks.

My mind tugging at its traces,
I see him in more dapper days
Outside the Kibble Palace
With my grandfather, having
His snapshot taken; men firing
That year's leaves.
The Gardens are only a stone's throw
From where I live . . . But now
A younger self comes clutching at my sleeve.

Or off to Innellan, singing, we would go,
Boarding the steamer at the Broomielaw
In broad summer, these boomps-a-daisy
Days, the ship's band playing in a lazy

Swell, my father steering well clear
Of the bar, mother making neat
Packets of waste-paper to carry
To the nearest basket or (more likely)
All the way back to Cranworth Street.

Leaving my father at it
(He'd rather be alone) I take
My mother through the changed Botanics.
The bandstand is gone, and the great
Rain-barrels that used to rot
And overflow. Everything is neat
And plastic. And it is I who must walk
Slowly for her, past the sludge
And pocked marble of Queen Margaret Bridge.

To My Father

One of my earliest memories (remember
Those Capone hats, the polka-dot ties)
Is of the late thirties: posing
With yourself and grandfather before
The park railings; me dribbling
Ice-cream, you so spick and smiling
The congregation never imagined
How little you made. Three generations,
In the palm of a hand. A year later
Grandfather died. War was declared.

In '42 we motored to Kilmarnock
In Alec Martin's Terraplane Hudson.
We found a pond, and six goldfish
Blurred under ice. They survived
That winter, but a gull got them in the end.
Each year we picnicked on the lawn;
Mother crooking her finger
As she sipped her lime. When
They carried you out on a stretcher
She knew you'd never preach again.

Since you retired, we've seen more
Of each other. Yet I spend this forenoon
Typing, to bring you closer—when
We could have been together. Part of what
I dread is that clear mind nodding

Before its flickering screen. If we come over
Tonight, there will be the added irony
Of proving my visit isn't out of duty
When, to myself, I doubt the dignity
Of a love comprising so much guilt and pity.

Reiteration

What terrifies me is that you should see your death
Reflected in my eyes. Yours are moist, glazed
Over; rimmed with red, as you gaze
At the images on their tiny screen. Beneath

The surface of things, your heart takes
Irregular leaps forward, toward the dark.
Its rhythms are broken easily; by the van parked
Too close for comfort, the fool whose brakes

Took him through the Argyle Street
Lights; Lennox's goal in the dying minutes . . .
And I think of the pressures youth puts
On age, neither prepared to meet

The other half-way. I remember you beat
Me, with a leather belt, for using a word
That can nowadays be overheard
Even in your trim Bearsden street.

I swore I'd get my own back
When I was older, stronger:
I'd wait till you no longer
Had the upper hand, and give you an attack

One way or another. Now I see
How strengths vary; the grasp
Of one over another depending not on the clasp
Of wrist or forearm. You are still stronger than me—

And apart from all else, have more experience
Of death's ways, having watched others go.
Here in this tiny space, you
Stare calmly at what I only dimly sense.

Far from being imprisoned in this room,
Which is how I'd seen it, the big guns
Thudding, I realise you've won
More battles than most—and have just one to come.

Climber

I set out, the shale patchwork dull
Below me, but seeing clearly what lies ahead:
The spiral, its bracelet of jet.
                             The reservoir
Tilts, a facet of the eye.
                             I remember playing
Steeplejacks, splaying the rotunda, toes cramped
By space. This is the real thing. I straddle
A spur. Cold cockerel, my world spins!

Message from an Island

The air here is so rarified, it seems
I have no shape—there being no substance
To contain me. Even when definition occurs,
There is nothing to show where I have been:
The heather is pliant; lochans open,
Black primroses, at my feet. How much worse
In winter, the dunes like bison; the mind

Stitched to its hammock, drifting further in.
Though my coming here is part voluntary,
I cannot thrive on this vocabulary
Of isolation. Unless I return
To the mainland with its proven means
Of communication, I shall end up tapping
On stone, holding flint to the sun.

Shirt strung on a pole, I scan the horizon.
I must seal my message in a bottle of its own.
The tide swills past Rodil. The sun
Is a red flare, a crate of oranges smashed
By the green Atlantic. The images come:
The remains of women and children, lashed
Together and thrown into the Mekong . . .

On their way out to sea, they pass my island,
That charmed circle where I have no need
To fight for survival at such a level:
I cannot imagine what it is like to be under fire,
To flee from the volcano as lava pours;

To watch literal murderers approach, visible
Axe-blades descend. Yet we are all part

Of one another. It is up to me to get
My message through. So far I have been defeated
By the tide. As I throw this bottle in,
I realise it may land with the others
On the rocks below. Meanwhile
The darkness gathers and swivels
Towards me, the barrel of a great gun.

At Coruisk

1

Think of it: a honeymoon at the foot
Of the Cuillin, and not once to see them
For mist—till on the last day we broached
From Elgol the seven crowned kings.

So intense the experience: not summers only,
But years, cramming one afternoon—
Thus keenly the glimpse awaited.
Nor had been envisaged such blueness:

Ice-crests mirrored in Coruisk, blue
Upon blue, as we followed
The path home. The moon crescent.
The sky, powdered flint.

2

Tempting to see these things
As manifestations of the mind
Significant through ourselves,
Which precede and succeed our notice.

For all that, the shadows are real.
They darken or illumine, at will;
Are points from which
To examine ourselves. But watch

How you go: yonder are scurrs
Would cut you down; nearer
To hand, rusty bracken,
Peat-holes where you'd cramp and drown.

3
So we get to know landscape,
And each other, better;
Our breathing filling the air
With each lap tackled. We learn

That the end of the road is seldom
A given point; that bridges exist
Too narrow to be crossed
More than two abreast.

Yet remains the fear, when
We look round, that two figures
Not dissimilar to ourselves should appear
Transparent, then vanish altogether.

Limits

Under Roneval
Not from Tiumpan Head or the white sands of Lewis
Do I blare my love, but let it settle
In the lochs and crannies of South Harris.

There may well be guilt in this:
The trout leaping in these waters
Being secretive enough for my style.

Even at that I am perceived
By the buzzard on his ledge of glass,
The still heron on his stalk.

Movements
That night we met as whales do,
Or porpoises, in a breaking sea:

Bodies making contact, because
We could not help it. The tides
Disguising movement of muscle, fin.

Having taken what we could of one
Another, we moved off into our separate dark.

Loch Meurach
I cast into my peat-pool,
Wind and ripple right.
Telling myself I need food,
Not pleasure only. But after
Each plateful, I try for more.

So the events of this summer
Are transparencies, with you always
Just out of the picture—
Albeit safely (I tell myself)
In mind. How often

Does the eye precede
What the body intends
To fulfil? The rod jerks.
Instinctively, I reel in. I step
From the shallows. I make my kill.

Envoi
Leaving the Island we wallow,
Trough after trough, between Renish
And Lord MacDonald's Table.

Trying not to take in
The stack rising and falling, I concentrate
On keeping my stomach down. Elsewhere

You ride it out, your fashion.
Each swell solid
From Quiraing, the Cuillin:

The mind's distemper
Diverting the horror
Of those who drowned there.

Only when we are berthed together
May we take full measure
Of the charmed lives we bear.

Marriage a Mountain Ridge

1

Like most, one way or another, ours
Has been through some dark couloirs.

I cannot swear to actual crevasses—
But have sensed them underfoot. (One night

On Beinn Fhada I lost my footing, and was fortunate
A rowan took my weight.)

This way I am better equipped
For keeping, if not to the spirit, the letter.

Crampons and pitons fitted, we face
The next assault, roped together. I also carry

An ice-pick—but fear to use it,
Lest it sink too deeply in.

2

Perhaps the hardest lesson
Is to accept the Brocken,

The Man with the Rainbow, as stemming
From myself; a projection

Of my own form. The cauldron
Below me, thin air.

In these rarefied labyrinths
The way forward

Is to focus
On a fixed point;

One hand gripping firmly
Its moral thread.

3
Whether scaling Etive
Of the shifting faces,

Or on the summit of Blaven,
Sheet-ice glistening

Through walls of mist,
It is all one. The tracks

We pursue are ours;
The zone we would enter

Not the mountain, but ourselves.
So for a moment, the mind

May afford to swing out
Over the wide abyss.

4
Then comes the point when body
And mind are one, each indefinable

Except in terms of the other.
Head and heart held

In a single noose. The Beast,
The Grey Man, cannot touch us here.

His footprints descending,
Identical with our own.

Later, victims of Time and Loss,
We will return and gaze there—

And marvel at such heights
Conquered, such blazing air.